Childlike

Faith

Saying Yes to God

by

Porsha Deun

Devotion Books by Porsha Deun

Childlike Faith—Saying Yes to God

ISBN (paperback): 979-8-9901518-4-0

ISBN (eBook): 979-8-9901518-5-7

Dedication

To my Granny Baby & my late Granddaddy,
I could never thank God enough for blessing me to have
you two as grandparents.

Introduction

My Grandmother's Experiment

My grandmother used to play a game with me and my two brothers, a.k.a., Randy's kids. Well, to us it was a game, but it was a study, an experiment, on faith for my grandmother. Because we spent, let's say, a third of every week at our grandparents' house, we played this game often. Or should I say, our grandmother did this experiment on us often.

This was the experiment: me or one of my brothers would walk through the family room, minding our very childlike business, most likely coming from or going outside. "Come here," she'd say. "Let me bust your head open to the white meat."

Now, when hearing these words, one would take that as a threat to their life. *The white meat.* That means brain damage and possibly death. This is going to hurt, and not the "this is going to hurt me more than it hurts you" kind of hurt.

But you know what my brothers and I did each and every time this *threat* was dished out to us?

We laughed.

Let me pause here and tell you about our cousin that we call Boo. Boo is the same age as me, so we grew up together. He, too, was given this same *threat.* He didn't laugh when our grandmother said these words to him. Instead, he stood there and looked at her like she was crazy, and a very simple word came out of his mouth.

"No."

That was a logical response given the words said to him. There was absolutely nothing wrong with his response. He was protecting his person. Again, he was being logical.

My brothers and I were not being logical. Clearly.

Faith, even childlike faith, will take you where logic could and would never go.

Back to the experiment.

After laughing, whichever one of us Granny was experimenting on that day would happily walk over to her. She'd pat her thigh and say, "Lay your head right here."

We'd laugh some more. Keep in mind this was a *threat*, and we were laughing.

Childlike faith.

We'd lay our head in her lap, still giggling. Granny would place one hand on our head and gently come down with her other hand, *busting our heads open*, but really, she was hitting her own hand. Granny even had a "wham, wham, wham" sound effect she'd do with it.

All involved were laughing all the while.

We, Randy's kids, could laugh about it because the threat came from our grandmother. Not because she was a softy. Trust me, she was and is not. But it was because we had faith in who she was. We had faith that even if *the white meat* was hanging out of our head, we were going to be just fine.

My brothers and I would get up like we just played our favorite game with one of our favorite persons in the world, because we had. This was our special game with our grandmother.

Childlike faith.

This is the type of faith the Lord wants us to walk around with, no matter what we are facing. Your special relationship with God should bring out childlike faith in you.

Matthew 18:2-5 states:

And Jesus called a little child unto him and set him in the midst of them and said, Verily I say unto you, except ye be converted and become as little children, ye shall not enter into the kingdom of heaven. Whosoever therefore shall humble himself as this little child, the same is greatest in the kingdom of heaven. And whoso shall receive on such little child in my name receiveth me. (KJV)

I know that when this passage is discussed and taught, all people see there is the child being humble. That is understandable since the word is right there in the scripture. Let me say this to you: it takes great faith, childlike faith even, to be humble. It simply is not possible to humble yourself before a greater power in which you have no faith in. Faith and humility go hand-in-hand. One cannot exist without the other.

And without faith, you cannot please God (Hebrews 11:6).

The focus of this devotion will be Matthew 18:3, becoming as a little child to enter the kingdom of heaven. The child gave Jesus no protest in coming to Him, in being the focal point of the lesson He was teaching His followers.

Childlike faith.

Here is another example of childlike faith that most people would be familiar with. Have you ever had a child argue you down over the validity of Santa Claus or the tooth fairy? These babies are serious, sometimes to the point of tears, in trying to prove that their favorite figures, taught to them by their families and society, are as real as you and me. I mean, they really believe in them. That's why they write letters to the North Pole for their wishes that year and put their recently loosed tooth under the pillow, hoping to receive a few dollars.

They are displaying childlike faith.

Throughout the rest of this book, we will look at examples of childlike faith being displayed in Scripture. There are also blank pages for your reflection with prompts on what to journal on the pages. If you are reading the ebook version of this, sorry, it doesn't have the blank pages, but I would suggest dedicating a small journal just for this. Before we get into the heart of this devotion, please use the blank pages after this introduction to reflect on times in your life you've displayed childlike faith. If you can't think of your own experience, use one you've witnessed or one from

Scripture. How can you let this experience influence your daily actions?

_____

_____

_____

_____

_____

_____

_____

_____

_____

_____

The Unnamed Child

Faith of the Unknown Child

There are plenty of examples of childlike faith throughout Scripture.

One of my favorite examples is of a boy whose name wasn't provided in the Bible. All four Gospels tell the story of Jesus feeding the multitude of 5,000 men, plus women and children, with two fish and five loaves of bread. It was a modest lunch for a child. When this miracle is discussed, often the focus is on Jesus doing what only He could do, or the lack of faith of the disciples, the men Jesus chose to lead the charge of spreading the gospel after His resurrection. Very little attention is given to the boy. There is no mention of the boy's family being there. If they'd been there, I'd imagine they would have said something to Andrew when he volunteered the meal that was enough to feed one, maybe two people. I know a parent or two (or even an auntie like myself) who would have pressed Andrew about his audacity.

The boy could have run away with his meal. It would have been so easy for him to dart into the crowd, lost to the disciples and Jesus. After all, they were *taking* from him. Neither Matthew, Mark, Luke, nor John mentions the boy protesting or doing what we adults do too often, telling Jesus "no". He gave up his meal without a fight, and the Lord gave thanks and multiplied the modest meal. Everyone in attendance was blessed because of it. The boy's cup ran over that day onto everyone else.

Childlike faith blessed thousands of people and proved Jesus to be the Son of God. When you have childlike faith, it makes space for God to move in your life in a way that only He can. Jesus showed right then and there that by giving whatever you have, whatever you've been carrying, over to God, He will take it and do exceeding abundantly above all you could ask or think (Eph 3:20)

What is it you've been telling the Lord no on?

What has God asked of you that has you hiding in the crowd like Adam and Eve hid in the bushes?

Take a moment to reflect on this on the blank pages at the end of this chapter. How much more freeing would it be to hand whatever you are carrying over to God the way this unnamed boy handed his meager meal to Jesus?

Let's look at an instance of a child letting their faith allow God to give them and others the victory.

A Child Answering God's Call

Faith of Samuel

In 1 Samuel 3, a boy named Samuel was being raised by the high priest Eli. The chapter describes how the Lord called on Samuel one night, and Samuel, being a child and not knowing the sound of God's voice, thought it was Eli calling him. This happened three times. When Eli realized what was happening, he instructed Samuel on how to respond.

> *Therefore Eli said unto Samuel, Go, lie down;*
> *and it shall be, if he call thee, that though*
> *shalt say, Speak, Lord; for thy servant*

heareth. So Samuel went and lay down in his place. (vs. 9, KJV)

Samuel did exactly what Eli instructed him to do. His obedience was a manifestation of his faith. Samuel did not know who was calling him, nor the reason he was being called, but he answered anyway.

Again, what have you been ignoring or telling God no about? Just because you don't have all the answers and can't see the full picture doesn't mean you don't need to tell God yes. Remember, God doesn't owe you a full explanation. Your growth, your freedom, your peace of mind, your elevation, are all of life support. Why not try faith, especially when logic fails? The children of Isreal wandered in the wilderness for 40 years because of their lack of faith and obedience. God is waiting for you to act right.

Samuel, a child, told God yes, and the Lord gave him a word. Even though that word was not necessarily one of glad tidings, it established Samuel as a great prophet, as everything God told him came forth.

Sister, Brother, say yes to God and let Him establish you. Get your stubbornness, questioning, and double-mindedness out of the way so that you can bear His fruit. You do not know what God's plans for you are. Neither did the child, Samuel. That child didn't know that one day he would name the first king of Isreal and would have an intricate role in establishing the earthly kingdom that Jesus will later rule. Still not knowing God's plans for his life, Samuel had a childlike faith that God would continue to guide him even after the death of his mentor, Eli.

Afterwards, let's look at another instance of a child letting their faith make room for God to do something grown men were too afraid to do.

In the blank space below, name the things you've told God no about. Go back as far as you want. Be honest with yourself. The purpose of this is not for you to beat yourself up over it. You've already asked for forgiveness in the last chapter. This is to put a name to where we messed up so that we know what it looks like when we lose our faith, so that we don't do that again.

_____

_____

_____

_____

_____

_____

_____

_____

A Child Doing What Men Were Too Afraid to Do

Faith of David

Even if you didn't grow up in church, you know the story of David and Goliath. Young shepherd boy David had the faith that a bunch of grown men with swords and shields did not. First, I want to look at the faith David showed before he was in position to see Goliath.

David was minding his shepherd boy business out in the field when his father, Jesse, called for him. Jesse gave David very specific instructions. In 1 Samuel 17:17, Jesse tells David to take some provisions (corn, bread, and cheese) to the camp where his older brothers were on the battlefield and to return to him with a report on how his brothers and the war are doing.

Hear me when I say this. No one, no human, can ask me to go into an active war zone for anything. ANYTHING. Clearly, I'm not David, but I digress.

David obeyed his father. Obedience is your faith in action. By obeying his father, David, in action, showed that he had faith he'd not only make it to his brothers, but he'd be able to get back to Jesse to give the report.

That thing God has been telling you to do, whether it is putting your skills and talents to use at your church home, starting the ministry, the business, that Word to share with someone else…why do you not have the faith, the childlike faith, that if God gave you the instructions, then you CAN do exactly what He said you could? Your obedience is a requirement. This faith thing is not optional on your Christian walk.

This is why young David is such a good example of childlike faith. In following the instructions of his father, as we should of our heavenly Father, it led him to the greatest defeat prior to Jesus' triumph over death. With a slingshot made of a long piece of leather, he was able not only to take down Goliath, but he confirmed and solidified his future as the second king of Isreal and Judah.

Pay attention to this. When David set out to do as his father told him, he had no idea that he'd be going to the war to fight, let alone winning it. All he did was go where he was told, and he ended up doing so much more.

Had David disobeyed his father, not had childlike faith, Isreal would've been captured by the Philistines, he would never have become king, Solomon is never born, and the prophesied genealogy of Jesus would not have proven true. Generations, the entire world for that matter, would've been forever changed. Doomed.

Your expression of your childlike faith, your obedience to God, is so much bigger than you.

On the lined pages at the end of this chapter, reflect on that thing God nudged you to do that you hesitated on and now someone else is doing it and doing it well. Or that move (physically or spiritually) you know God told you to do, and you ended hitting your version of Jonah's whale for not being obedient. We are to be God's instruments and have faith that His will and desire for us is truly good. Have an honest conversation with God about it and earnestly ask Him to show you how you should move forward.

_____

_____

_____

_____

Not Letting God Go

The Faith of Jacob

How, as adults, can we have and express childlike faith? Afterall, we've lived lives. We're jaded, hurt, mentally and emotionally exhausted, depressed, anxious, and have little patience. The Scriptures have examples of adults showing childlike faith, too.

Have you ever had a child decide they were going to hold on to you by any means necessary? It's like they grow extra arms and legs. You just can't get free! While they are laughing like it's a game, you're hot, sweating, and panting, and they STILL have hold of you.

Jacob displayed childlike faith when he wrestled with the Lord and declared that he wasn't turning the Lord loose until He blessed him (Gen 32:24-30).

How tight is your spiritual grip on God? Is your faith large enough to tell God, "I'm not letting go until You bless me?"

Keep this in mind. Even though Jacob *physically* let the Lord go, he still held him close to his heart. We need to desire God, to hold Him in our hearts. James 4:8 states:

> *Draw nigh to God, and he will draw nigh to you. Cleanse your hands, ye sinners; and purify your hearts, ye double minded.*

Jacob, even in his messy marriages, favoritism as a parent, scheming against his brother, grief, and stubbornness, still desired to follow God. The same can be said about David with his lust, scheming, and lying. In all of his sin, David's earnest desire was always towards God, and God declared him to have a heart after His own.

No one mentioned in this book, outside of God the Father and God the Son, are perfect beings. You aren't perfect, and you don't have to be. God knew exactly who He was getting when He called you for what He called you for.

Let me say that again.

God knew exactly who He was getting when He called you for what He called you for.

Peter was a hothead. Matthew worked for the Roman government, which was oppressing his people. Mary Magdelene was plagued with demons. Moses was a murderer. Abraham was a liar. Jacob was deceitful. Paul was a persecutor of any and everyone who followed Christ.

You are you. God still called you. He still chose you. He still loves you.

Where is your faith? Where is your 'yes' to God?

On the lined area at the end of this chapter, make your own declaration to God about not letting Him go, and thank Him for never letting you go.

_____

_____

_____

_____

_____

_____

_____

Believing God Will Answer Your Request

The Faith of Peter

Another instance of childlike faith on display in an adult is Peter asking Jesus to call him out onto the water (Matthew 14:28-31). This is probably, in my humble opinion, one of the best displays of "ask and ye shall receive" in all of Scripture.

Peter had the childlike faith to boldly ask Jesus to call him out to Him on the water. What is even better is that Jesus gave Peter exactly what he asked for. Peter walked on the water.

But then, Peter does something most humans do when they ask God for something, and He gives it to them. We often have the faith that God will give us what we request of Him, but lack the faith that God has also given us everything to keep said thing. Trees and waves are moving from the power of the wind (distractions and opposition) so much so that Peter (and we) forgot about the power of God. Jesus was right there on the water with Peter. The Lord watched in real time as fear replaced Peter's bold, childlike faith.

Jesus was right there, and Peter lost his faith in an instant, like he didn't grow up reading and hearing about God the Father parting the Red Sea so that the people of Isreal could walk on dry land, leaving footprints where no human had ever walked before or since. Peter lost faith after getting exactly what he asked for, and he began to sink.

This is my favorite part of the story. Jesus is not a helicopter Savior.

He stands there and watches. Jesus watches as Peter initially acts on the faith. He witnesses Peter take his eyes (mind) off Him and give more attention to everything else around him. Jesus watches him sink into the sea, with full knowledge that humans can't breathe under water. He watches as Peter practically gives himself over to the clutches of death.

That is until Peter calls out to him. "Lord, save me (vs. 30)."

Peter is the only other person to have walked on water. When Jesus said "come" in verse 29, it was not just a handout or gift or answered prayer. It was a welcome, a stepping stone, a building block, an invitation to a higher level of faith. God giving you what you asked for requires more faith from you in order to maintain said answered prayer. When God answers your prayer, He also gives you what you need to keep what you asked for. You just have to maintain your faith so it can be built upon and keep your focus on Him.

Can you imagine if Peter had kept his faith in that moment? How that would have inspired and grown the faith of the other disciples watching in the boat. Had Peter kept his focus on Jesus, it could have been a party of 13 men praising God in song and dance out there on that stormy sea.

When you make your requests of God or finally say *yes* to His calling for your life, childlike faith is required. It is a muscle that you will have to continually exercise and express with your obedience to His will.

Don't be like Peter at that moment. Taking your eyes off the Lord is not an option in this Christian walk. Don't let worldly influences replace your childlike faith, especially when Jesus said He would always be with us.

Remember, Jesus was right there in front of Peter. I imagine Jesus watching Peter sink and thinking, *how dumb can you be? I'M RIGHT HERE! Why are you concerned with anything else?*

This is how I translate the nine words Jesus said to him in verse 31.

> *And immediately, Jesus stretched forth his hand, and caught him, and said unto him,* **O thou of little faith, wherefore didst thou doubt?**

If you are going to ask God for something, have faith that He will give it to you **and** equip you with what you need to maintain and nurture it. All you have to do is keep your eyes on him. Use the lined space below to reflect on where you want to be and what you want God to do in your life (please don't make this materialistic).

Faith In The Unknown

Faith of Ruth

Hebrews 11 states that faith is the substance of things hoped for, the evidence of things unseen. To me personally, there is no greater example of this than Ruth. She was a Moabite woman who married into a then-wealthy Israelite family when she married the son of Naomi and Elimelek. If Ruth knew anything about the history of Israel, she knew the Israelites looked down on her. God commanded the Israelites not to mingle with the Moabites. The Moabites spoke a different tongue, worshiped false gods, had different customs, were of a different ethnicity, and may even have had a different skin tone that just wasn't seen among the Israelites of that time.

Yet, after the deaths of her husband, her brother-in-law, and her father-in-law, she decided to stay with her mother-in-law, Naomi. Ruth made a declaration, a vow, to Naomi when Naomi instructed Ruth to go back to her people.

> *But Ruth replies, "Don't urge me to leave you or to turn back from you. Where you go, I will go, and where you stay, I will stay. Your people will be my people and your God my God. Where you die, I will die, and there I will be buried. May the Lord deal with me, be it ever so severely, if even death separates you and me. (Ruth 1:16-17)"*

What a declaration! The only thing Ruth had seen of God was through her in-laws. This is why it is so important to bear the fruits of the Spirit at all times, because someone can be brought to God just by simply watching and observing you.

Again, everything about Israel and the one true living God was foreign to Ruth. The only thing she could expect from going with Naomi on her return to Bethlehem was that she'd be an outcast, even discriminated against. She didn't let that stop her.

Women, especially Black and women of Color, hear this: Ruth didn't let being "othered" stop her.

She had faith in a God she didn't grow up worshipping; faith in a God that told one group of people to stay away from her and her people. How tremendous is that?

Some of us (and yes, I'm including myself because I was once in this boat) grew up in the church and don't have that much faith in God, and we've known Him and His works all our lives.

Let that sink in.

Where is your faith in God?

Nothing but the Holy Spirit led Ruth to make such a declaration and to express such faith. Again, faith is expressed through obedience. Through the little bit of God she'd seen in her mother-in-law and father-in-law, Ruth had enough faith to follow the instructions God stirred in her spirit to turn her back on her family, her people, her land, her customs, and the gods she'd known all her life to go with Naomi, a woman she no longer had any obligations to. Ruth expressed that faith not only by going with Naomi but also by going to work to provide for herself and her mother-in-law, knowing there was a chance she wouldn't find favor anywhere simply because of who she was.

But the favor of God was with her, and now she is in the lineage of our Lord and Savior, Jesus Christ.

Ruth had no certainty of what was on the other side of the 'yes' to the God she did not know. You know

Him, and you should know there's always greater for you when you follow God.

Are you ready to say yes? On the lined spaces below, write out the things you're going to tell God 'yes' to.

_____

_____

_____

_____

_____

_____

_____

_____

What About You?

When was the last time you said 'yes' to the move, the apology, to the alms (offering), the business, and/or the giving of your talents in service to Him and others when the Spirit moved you to do so? We tell God 'no' on a daily basis and have absolutely no business doing so, especially considering all that He has already given us both here on Earth and in Eternity with Him.

Whatever it is God has put on your heart, please, for your own sake, tell Him 'yes'. God will force nothing on you, not even blessings of abundance. You must do your part by having childlike faith in Him and His divine plan for your life to say the most important part (at least to me) of the Model Prayer that Jesus gave to His disciples in Matthew 6:10:

> *...Thy will be done...*

For someone who is a follower of Christ, those of us who proclaim to be purchased by His blood, these are the four most powerful words we can say to God. And guess what? He wants to hear it from us. Not just when we need Him to come through for us on something or when we are at our wit's end, but daily. God desires to move in and throughout our lives every single day. How do I know that? Later in the same chapter of Matthew, Jesus drops this gem:

> *Vs. 33: But seek ye first the kingdom of God, and his righteousness; and **all these things shall be added unto you.***

If God didn't desire to move in our lives, Jesus wouldn't have given us the instruction to seek Him first.

In seeking Him, it opens us up for God's power to move in our lives, for His love, joy, forgiveness, and kindness to show to others through us. Seeking God makes space for Him to strengthen us during our long-suffering and gives us peace and the ability to be peaceful to others, no matter our situation. Through His work in us, we can be examples of faith, meekness, and temperance for others. These are the fruits of the Spirit the Apostle Paul states we must exemplify in Galatians 5:22-23.

Please don't let where you are in your Christian-walk hold your faith back. It doesn't matter how long you've been saved or how old or young you are. When God called the prophet Jeremiah, Jeremiah told God he couldn't speak to the nations because he was a child (Jeremiah 1:6). Do you know how God responded?

> *But the Lord said unto me, Say not, I am a*
> *child: for thou shalt go to all that I send thee,*
> *and whatsoever I command thee though*

shalt speak. Be not afraid of their faces: for I am with thee to deliver thee, saith the Lord. Then the Lord put forth his hand and touched my mouth. And the Lord said unto me, Behold, I have put my words in thy mouth.

You are also never too old to answer God's call. When Noah comes up at the end of Genesis 5, he is 500 years old. Noah expressed his faith by being obedient to what God told him to do (Gen 6:22). Keep in mind, rain, water falling from the clouds, was a foreign concept to everyone living until the first raindrop fell in Genesis 7. Noah had never seen or heard of rain prior to that. But he had faith that God would do exactly what He said He'd do.

Could you imagine if Noah hadn't obeyed God? None of us would be here. This book would never have existed. Jesus wouldn't have been born, let alone crucified for our sins. There would be no path to salvation.

Again, your yes to God is so much bigger than you.

I want to challenge you to do something. As I previously mentioned, we tell God 'no' every day. I challenge you to say yes to at least one thing every single day. That person on the corner with a sign. Put some money in their hands without judging them or thinking of what they will do with it. Join that team/ministry at church. Give someone you don't know an encouraging word. Forgive the person who refuses to apologize. Pray for the person you don't like. Say yes to doing something for your health. 'Yes' to reading a chapter of Scripture instead of endlessly scrolling on social media or doing something that only temporarily satisfies your flesh. Say 'yes' to celibacy if you are unmarried. 'Yes' to serving each other if you are married. Say 'yes' to loving more wholeheartedly. 'Yes' to therapy because, yes, you need emotional healing, too. Say 'yes' to being kinder.

Say yes to God. Express your childlike faith. Writing and publishing this book is my expression of my childlike faith. I can't wait to see you express yours.

_____

_____

_____

_____

_____

_____

_____

_____

_____

_____

A Note from the Author:

Thank you for reading my book! I feel honored, truly.

Did you enjoy **Childlike Faith**? Be sure to leave a review everywhere you can!

This book was not easy for me to write. As I stated previously, my other books fall into the romance, erotica, and children's books categories. When I started writing, I never imagined the Lord would put it upon my heart to write a devotion. If you had told me that back in 2015, I would have laughed (I was working on a steamy romance then). I wasn't as spiritually mature then as I am now, and I still have plenty of growing to do.

Another challenge I had with this book was that my brother, a minister, is also working on his first book, a Scripture-based book on growing your business. Also, during the last bit of me working on this, he was leading a Bible study series titled *Unshakable Faith.* Though many of the examples I used had not come up during his study (as of the time I'm writing this), I was worried that people would think I was crossing over into his lane or using the class he leads for my book. I will pull this one thing from his class. To have *unshakable faith*, your faith has to be bigger than your feelings and fear. We often credit kids with being fearless, but really, their faith is limitless.

There were many days I did not work on this book because I was letting my feelings be bigger than my fear. I could've had this book done in a month had I not done that. Even as I am writing this, I want to be curled up under my electric blanket (it's currently the end of June and my a.c. works well) watching a yard makeover video on the red video channel, not at my desk typing away to *Hard Faught Hallelujah* by Brandon Lake & Jelly Roll on repeat. So, hear me when I say this book is just as much for me as it is for you.

Your faith does not care about your feelings, so don't let your feelings determine your faith.

Be blessed, beloved,

Porsha